Selected Poems of John Drinkwater

John Drinkwater

Selected Poems
of John Drinkwater

London
Sidgwick & Jackson, Ltd.
3 Adam St., W.C. 2
1922

Contents

A Prayer

LORD, not for light in darkness do we pray,
　　Not that the veil be lifted from our eyes,
Nor that the slow ascension of our day
　　　　Be otherwise.

Not for a clearer vision of the things
Whereof the fashioning shall make us great,
Not for remission of the peril and stings
　　　　Of time and fate.

Not for a fuller knowledge of the end
Whereto we travel, bruised yet unafraid,
Nor that the little healing that we lend
　　　　Shall be repaid.

Not these, O Lord.　We would not break the bars
Thy wisdom sets about us; we shall climb
Unfettered to the secrets of the stars
　　　　In Thy good time.

We do not crave the high perception swift
When to refrain were well, and when fulfil,
Nor yet the understanding strong to sift
　　　　The good from ill.

7

Not these, O Lord. For these Thou hast revealed,
We know the golden season when to reap
The heavy-fruited treasure of the field,
      The hour to sleep.

Not these. We know the hemlock from the rose,
The pure from stained, the noble from the base,
The tranquil holy light of truth that glows
      On Pity's face.

We know the paths wherein our feet should press,
Across our hearts are written Thy decrees,
Yet now, O Lord, be merciful to bless
      With more than these.

Grant us the will to fashion as we feel,
Grant us the strength to labour as we know,
Grant us the purpose, ribbed and edged with steel,
      To strike the blow.

Knowledge we ask not—knowledge Thou hast lent,
But, Lord, the will—there lies our bitter need,
Give us to build above the deep intent
      The deed, the deed.

Reckoning

I HEARD my love go laughing
    Beyond the bolted door,
I saw my love go riding
    Across the windy moor,
And I would give my love no word
Because of evil tales I heard.

Let fancy men go laughing,
    Let light men ride away,
Bruised corn is not for my mill,
    What's paid I will not pay,—
And so I thought because of this
Gossip that poisoned clasp and kiss.

Four hundred men went riding,
    And he the best of all,
A jolly man for labour,
    A sinewy man and tall ;
I watched him go beyond the hill,
And shaped my anger with my will.

At night my love came riding
    Across the dusky moor,
And other two rode with him
    Who knocked my bolted door,

And called me out and bade me see
How quiet a man a man could be.

And now the tales that stung me
  And gave my pride its rule,
Are worth a beggar's broken shoe
  Or the sermon of a fool,
And all I know and all I can
Is, false or true, he was my man.

Pierrot

Pierrot alone,
And then Pierrette,
And then a story to forget.

Pierrot alone.
Pierrette among the apple boughs,
Come down and take a Pierrot's kiss,
The moon is white upon your brows,
Pierrette among the apple boughs,
Your lips are cold, and I would set
A rose upon your lips, Pierrette,
A rosy kiss,
Pierrette, Pierrette.

And then Pierrette.
I've left my apple boughs, Pierrot,
A shadow now is on my face,
But still my lips are cold, and O
No rose is on my lips, Pierrot,
You laugh, and then you pass away
Among the scented leaves of May,
And on my face
The shadows stay.

And then a story to forget.
The petals fall upon the grass,
And I am crying in the dark,
The clouds above the white moon pass—
My tears are falling on the grass ;
Pierrot, Pierrot, I heard your vows
And left my blossomed apple boughs,
And sorrows dark
Are on my brows.

The Miracle

COME, sweetheart, listen, for I have a thing
 Most wonderful to tell you—news of spring.

Albeit winter still is in the air,
And the earth troubled, and the branches bare,

Yet down the fields to-day I saw her pass—
The spring—her feet went shining through the
 grass.

She touched the ragged hedgerows—I have seen
Her finger-prints, most delicately green ;

And she has whispered to the crocus leaves,
And to the garrulous sparrows in the eaves.

Swiftly she passed and shyly, and her fair
Young face was hidden in her cloudy hair.

She would not stay, her season is not yet,
But she has reawakened, and has set

The sap of all the world astir, and rent
Once more the shadows of our discontent.

Triumphant news—a miracle I sing—
The everlasting miracle of spring.

The Crowning of Dreaming John

I

SEVEN days he travelled
  Down the roads of England,
Out of leafy Warwick lanes
Into London Town.
Grey and very wrinkled
Was Dreaming John of Grafton,
But seven days he walked to see
A king put on his crown.

Down the streets of London
He asked the crowded people
Where would be the crowning
And when would it begin.
He said he'd got a shilling,
A shining silver shilling,
But when he came to Westminster
They wouldn't let him in.

Dreaming John of Grafton
Looked upon the people,
Laughed a little laugh, and then
Whistled and was gone.

Out along the long roads,
The twisting roads of England,
Back into the Warwick lanes
Wandered Dreaming John.

II

As twilight touched with her ghostly fingers
All the meadows and mellow hills,
And the great sun swept in his robes of glory—
Woven of petals of daffodils
And jewelled and fringed with leaves of the roses·
Down the plains of the western way,
Among the rows of the scented clover
Dreaming John in his dreaming lay.

Since dawn had folded the stars of heaven
He'd counted a score of miles and five,
And now, with a vagabond heart untroubled
And proud as the properest man alive,
He sat him down with a limber spirit
That all men covet and few may keep,

15

And he watched the summer draw round her
    beauty
The shadow that shepherds the world to sleep.

And up from the valleys and shining rivers,
And out of the shadowy wood-ways wild,
And down from the secret hills, and streaming
Out of the shimmering undefiled
Wonder of sky that arched him over,
Came a company shod in gold
And girt in gowns of a thousand blossoms,
Laughing and rainbow-aureoled.

Wrinkled and grey and with eyes a-wonder
And soul beatified, Dreaming John
Watched the marvellous company gather
While over the clover a glory shone;
They bore on their brows the hues of heaven,
Their limbs were sweet with flowers of the fields,
And their feet were bright with the gleaming
    treasure
That prodigal earth to her children yields.

They stood before him, and John was laughing
As they were laughing; he knew them all,
Spirits of trees and pools and meadows,
Mountain and windy waterfall,
Spirits of clouds and skies and rivers,
Leaves and shadows and rain and sun,
A crowded, jostling, laughing army,
And Dreaming John knew every one.

Among them then was a sound of singing
And chiming music, as one came down
The level rows of the scented clover,
Bearing aloft a flashing crown;
No word of a man's desert was spoken,
Nor any word of a man's unworth,
But there on the wrinkled brow it rested,
And Dreaming John was king of the earth.

Dreaming John of Grafton
Went away to London,
Saw the coloured banners fly,
Heard the great bells ring,
But though his tongue was civil
And he had a silver shilling,
They wouldn't let him in to see
The crowning of the King.

So back along the long roads,
The leafy roads of England,
Dreaming John went carolling,
Travelling alone,
And in a summer evening,
Among the scented clover,
He held before a shouting throng
A crowning of his own.

The Vagabond

I KNOW the pools where the grayling rise,
   I know the trees where the filberts fall,
I know the woods where the red fox lies,
   The twisted elms where the brown owls call.
And I've seldom a shilling to call my own,
   And there's never a girl I'd marry,
I thank the Lord I'm a rolling stone
   With never a care to carry.

I talk to the stars as they come and go
   On every night from July to June,
I'm free of the speech of the winds that blow,
   And I know what weather will sing what tune
I sow no seed and I pay no rent,
   And I thank no man for his bounties,
But I've a treasure that's never spent,
   I'm lord of a dozen counties.

In Lady Street

ALL day long the traffic goes
In Lady Street by dingy rows
Of sloven houses, tattered shops—
Fried fish, old clothes and fortune-tellers—
Tall trams on silver-shining rails,
With grinding wheels and swaying tops,
And lorries with their corded bales,
And screeching cars. " Buy, buy ! " the sellers
Of rags and bones and sickening meat
Cry all day long in Lady Street.

And when the sunshine has its way
In Lady Street, then all the grey
Dull desolation grows in state
More dull and grey and desolate,
And the sun is a shamefast thing,
A lord not comely-housed, a god
Seeing what gods must blush to see,
A song where it is ill to sing,
And each gold ray despiteously
Lies like a gold ironic rod.

Yet one grey man in Lady Street
Looks for the sun.   He never bent
Life to his will, his travelling feet
Have scaled no cloudy continent,
Nor has the sickle-hand been strong.
He lives in Lady Street ; a bed,
Four cobwebbed walls

                But all day long
A time is singing in his head
Of youth in Gloucester lanes.   He hears
The wind among the barley-blades,
The tapping of the woodpeckers
On the smooth beeches, thistle-spades
Slicing the sinewy roots ; he sees
The hooded filberts in the copse
Beyond the loaded orchard trees,
The netted avenues of hops ;
He smells the honeysuckle thrown
Along the hedge.   He lives alone,
Alone—yet not alone, for sweet
Are Gloucester lanes in Lady Street.

Aye, Gloucester lanes   For down below
The cobwebbed room this grey man plies
A trade, a coloured trade.   A show
Of many-coloured merchandise

Is in his shop.　Brown filberts there,
And apples red with Gloucester air,
And cauliflowers he keeps, and round
Smooth marrows grown on Gloucester ground,
Fat cabbages and yellow plums,
And gaudy brave chrysanthemums.
And times a glossy pheasant lies
Among his store, not Tyrian dyes
More rich than are the neck-feathers ;
And times a prize of violets,
Or dewy mushrooms satin-skinned,
And times an unfamiliar wind
Robbed of its woodland favour stirs
Gay daffodils this grey man sets
Among his treasure.

　　　　　　　　All day long
In Lady Street the traffic goes
By dingy houses, desolate rows
Of shops that stare like hopeless eyes.
Day long the sellers cry their cries,
The fortune-tellers tell no wrong
Of lives that know not any right,
And drift, that has not even the will
To drift, toils through the day until
The wage of sleep is won at night.

But this grey man heeds not at all
The hell of Lady Street.   His stall
Of many-coloured merchandise
He makes a shining paradise,
As all day long chrysanthemums
He sells, and red and yellow plums
And cauliflowers.   In that one spot
Of Lady Street the sun is not
Ashamed to shine and send a rare
Shower of colour through the air ;
The grey man says the sun is sweet
On Gloucester lanes in Lady Street.

At Grafton

GOD laughed when he made Grafton
  That's under Bredon Hill,
A jewel in a jewelled plain.
The seasons work their will
On golden thatch and crumbling stone,
And every soft-lipped breeze
Makes music for the Grafton men
In comfortable trees.

God's beauty over Grafton
Stole into roof and wall,
And hallowed every pavèd path
And every lowly stall,
And to a woven wonder
Conspired with one accord
The labour of the servant,
The labour of the Lord.

And momently to Grafton
Comes in from vale and wold
The sound of sheep unshepherded,
The sound of sheep in fold,
And, blown along the bases
Of lands that set their wide
Frank brows to God, comes chanting
The breath of Bristol tide.

January Dusk

AUSTERE and clad in sombre robes of grey,
  With hands upfolded and with silent wings,
In unimpassioned mystery the day
  Passes; a lonely thrush its requiem sings.

The dust of night is tangled in the boughs
  Of leafless lime and lilac, and the pine
Grows blacker, and the star upon the brows
  Of sleep is set in heaven for a sign.

Earth's little weary peoples fall on peace
  And dream of breaking buds and blossoming,
Of primrose airs, of days of large increase,
  And all the coloured retinue of spring.

A Town Window

BEYOND my window in the night
    Is but a drab inglorious street,
Yet there the frost and clean starlight
    As over Warwick woods are sweet.

Under the grey drift of the town
    The crocus works among the mould
As eagerly as those that crown
    The Warwick spring in flame and gold.

And when the tramway down the hill
    Across the cobbles moans and rings,
There is about my window-sill
    The tumult of a thousand wings.

Last Confessional

FOR all ill words that I have spoken,
   For all clear moods that I have broken,
For all despite and hasty breath,
Forgive me, Love, forgive me, Death.

Death, master of the great assize,
Love, falling now to memories,
   You two alone I need to prove,
   Forgive me, Death, forgive me, Love.

For every tenderness undone,
For pride when holiness was none
   But only easy charity,
   O Death, be pardoner to me.

For stubborn thought that would not make
Measure of love's thought for love's sake,
   But kept a sullen difference,
   Take, Love, this laggard penitence.

For cloudy words too vainly spent
To prosper but in argument,
   When truth stood lonely at the gate,
   On your compassion, Death, I wait.

27

For all the beauty that escaped
This foolish brain, unsung, unshaped,
   For wonder that was slow to move,
   Forgive me, Death, forgive me, Love.

For love that kept a secret cruse,
For life defeated of its dues,
   This latest word of all my breath—
   Forgive me, Love, forgive me, Death.

Mad Tom Tatterman

"OLD man, grey man, good man scavenger,
    Bearing is it eighty years upon your
crumpled back ?
What is it you gather in the frosty weather,
    Is there any treasure here to carry in your
sack ?"

.   .   .   .

" I've a million acres and a thousand head of cattle,
And a foaming river where the silver salmon leap ;
But I've left fat valleys to dig in sullen alleys
    Just because a twisted star rode by me in my
sleep.

" I've a brain is dancing to an old forgotten music
    Heard when all the world was just a crazy flight
of dreams,
And don't you know I scatter in the dirt along the
gutter
    Seeds that little ladies nursed by Babylonian
streams ?

" Mad Tom Tatterman, that is how they call me.
    Oh, they know so much, so much, all so neatly
dressed ;

29

I've a tale to tell you—come and listen, will you ?—
  One as ragged as the twigs that make a magpie's
    nest.

" Ragged, oh, but very wise.   You and this and
    that man,
  All of you are making things that none of you
    would lack,
And so your eyes grow dusty, and so your limbs
    grow rusty.—
  But mad Tom Tatterman puts nothing in his
    sack.

" Nothing in my sack, sirs, but the Sea of Galilee
  Was walked for mad Tom Tatterman, and when
    I go to sleep
They'll know that I have driven through the acres
    of broad heaven
  Flocks are whiter than the flocks that all your
    shepherds keep."

Mamble

I NEVER went to Mamble
   That lies above the Teme,
So I wonder who's in Mamble,
And whether people seem
Who breed and brew along there
As lazy as the name,
And whether any song there
Sets alehouse wits aflame.

The finger-post says Mamble,
And that is all I know
Of the narrow road to Mamble,
And should I turn and go
To that place of lazy token
That lies above the Teme,
There might be a Mamble broken
That was lissom in a dream.

So leave the road to Mamble
And take another road
To as good a place as Mamble
Be it lazy as a toad ;

Who travels Worcester county
Takes any place that comes
When April tosses bounty
To the cherries and the plums.

Birthright

LORD RAMESES of Egypt sighed
   Because a summer evening passed ;
And little Ariadne cried
   That summer fancy fell at last
To dust ; and young Verona died
   When beauty's hour was overcast.

Theirs was the bitterness we know
   Because the clouds of hawthorn keep
So short a state, and kisses go
   To tombs unfathomably deep,
While Rameses and Romeo
   And little Ariadne sleep.

Olton Pools

(TO G. C. G.)

NOW June walks on the waters,
   And the cuckoo's last enchantment
Passes from Olton pools.

Now dawn comes to my window
Breathing midsummer roses,
And scythes are wet with dew.

Is it not strange for ever
That, bowered in this wonder,
Man keeps a jealous heart ? . . .

That June and the June waters,
And birds and dawn-lit roses,
Are gospels in the wind,

Fading upon the deserts,
Poor pilgrim revelations ? . . .
Hist . . . over Olton pools !

Sunrise on Rydal Water

(TO E. DE S.)

COME down at dawn from windless hills
 Into the valley of the lake,
Where yet a larger quiet fills
 The hour, and mist and water make
  With rocks and reeds and island boughs
  One silence and one element,
  Where wonder goes surely as once
  It went
   By Galilean prows.

Moveless the water and the mist,
 Moveless the secret air above,
Hushed as upon some happy tryst
 The poised expectancy of love ;
  What spirit is it that adores
  What mighty presence yet unseen ?
  What consummation works apace
  Between
   These rapt enchanted shores ?

Never did virgin beauty wake
 Devouter to the bridal feast
Than moves this hour upon the lake
 In adoration to the east ;

35

Here is the bride a god may know,
The primal will, the young consent,
Till surely upon the appointed mood
Intent
    The god shall leap—and, lo,

Over the lake's end strikes the sun,
  White, flameless fire; some purity
Thrilling the mist, a splendour won
  Out of the world's heart. Let there be
    Thoughts, and atonements, and desires,
    Proud limbs, and undeliberate tongue,
    Where now we move with mortal oars
    Among
      Immortal dews and fires.

So the old mating goes apace,
  Wind with the sea, and blood with thought,
Lover with lover; and the grace
  Of understanding comes unsought
    When stars into the twilight steer,
    Or thrushes build among the may,
    Or wonder moves between the hills,
    And day
      Comes up on Rydal mere.

Holiness

IF all the carts were painted gay,
  And all the streets swept clean,
And all the children came to play
  By hollyhocks, with green
  Grasses to grow between;

If all the houses looked as though
  Some heart were in their stones;
If all the people that we know
  Were dressed in scarlet gowns,
  With feathers in their crowns,

I think this gaiety would make
  A spiritual land.
I think that holiness would take
  This laughter by the hand,
  Till both should understand.

Anthony Crundle

Here lies the body of
ANTHONY CRUNDLE,
Farmer, of this parish,
Who died in 1849 at the age of 82.
" He delighted in music."
R.I.P.

And of
SUSAN,
For fifty-three years his wife,
Who died in 1860, aged 86.

ANTHONY CRUNDLE of Dorrington Wood
    Played on a piccolo. Lord was he,
For seventy years, of sheaves that stood
    Under the perry and cider tree;
    Anthony Crundle, R.I.P.

And because he prospered with sickle and scythe,
    With cattle afield and labouring ewe,
Anthony was uncommonly blithe,
    And played of a night to himself and Sue
    Anthony Crundle, eighty-two.

The earth to till, and a tune to play,
    And Susan for fifty years and three,
And Dorrington Wood at the end of day . . .
    May Providence do no worse by me;
    Anthony Crundle, R.I.P.

Immortality

WHEN other beauty governs other lips,
 And snowdrops come to strange and happy
  springs,
When seas renewed bear yet unbuilded ships,
 And alien hearts know all familiar things,
When frosty nights bring comrades to enjoy
 Sweet hours at hearths where we no longer sit,
When Liverpool is one with dusty Troy,
 And London famed as Attica for wit . . .
How shall it be with you, and you, and you,
 How with us all who have gone greatly here
In friendship, making some delight, some true
 Song in the dark, some story against fear?
Shall song still walk with love, and life be brave,
And we, who were all these, be but the grave?

No ; lovers yet shall tell the nightingale
   Sometimes a song that we of old time made,
And gossips gathered at the twilight ale
   Shall say, " Those two were friends," or,
     " Unafraid
Of bitter thought were those because they loved
   Better than most." And sometimes shall be told
How one, who died in his young beauty, moved,
   As Astrophel, those English hearts of old.
And the new seas shall take the new ships home
   Telling how yet the Dymock orchards stand,
And you shall walk with Julius at Rome,
   And Paul shall be my fellow in the Strand ;
There in the midst of all those words shall be
Our names, our ghosts, our immortality.

Petition

O LORD, I pray: that for each happiness
My housemate brings I may give back no less
    Than all my fertile will;

That I may take from friends but as the stream
Creates again the hawthorn bloom adream
    Above the river sill;

That I may see the spurge upon the wall
And hear the nesting birds give call to call,
    Keeping my wonder new;

That I may have a body fit to mate
With the green fields, and stars, and streams in
    spate,
    And clean as clover-dew;

That I may have the courage to confute
All fools with silence when they will dispute,
    All fools who will deride;

That I may know all strict and sinewy art
As that in man which is the counterpart,
    Lord, of Thy fiercest pride;

That somehow this beloved earth may wear
A later grace for all the love I bear,
      For some song that I sing ;

That, when I die, this word may stand for me—
He had a heart to praise, an eye to see,
      And beauty was his king.

May Garden

A SHOWER of green gems on my apple-tree
    This first morning of May
Has fallen out of the night, to be
    Herald of holiday—
Bright gems of green that, fallen there,
Seem fixed and glowing on the air.

Until a flutter of blackbird wings
    Shakes and makes the boughs alive,
And the gems are now no frozen things,
    But apple-green buds to thrive
On sap of my May garden, how well
The green September globes will tell.

Also my pear-tree has its buds,
    But they are silver yellow,
Like autumn meadows when the floods
    Are silver under willow,
And here shall long and shapely pears
Be gathered while the autumn wears.

And there are sixty daffodils
    Beneath my wall. . . .
And jealousy it is that kills
    This world when all
The spring's behaviour here is spent
To make the world magnificent.

Reciprocity

I DO not think that skies and meadows are
  Moral, or that the fixture of a star
Comes of a quiet spirit, or that trees
Have wisdom in their windless silences.
Yet these are things invested in my mood
With constancy, and peace, and fortitude,
That in my troubled season I can cry
Upon the wide composure of the sky,
And envy fields, and wish that I might be
As little daunted as a star or tree.

The Hours

THOSE hours are best when suddenly
  The voices of the world are still,
And in that quiet place is heard
The voice of one small singing bird,
Alone within his quiet tree;

When to one field that crowns a hill,
With but the sky for neighbourhood,
The crowding counties of my brain
Give all their riches, lake and plain,
Cornland and fell and pillared wood;
When in a hill-top acre, bare
For the seed's use, I am aware
Of all the beauty that an age
Of earth has taught my eyes to see;

When Pride and Generosity,
The Constant Heart and Evil Rage,
Affection and Desire, and all
The passions of experience
Are no more tabled in my mind,

45

Learning's idolatry, but find
Particularity of sense
In daily fortitudes that fall
From this or that companion,
Or in an angry gossip's word:

When one man speaks for Every One,
When Music lives in one small bird,
When in a furrowed hill we see
All beauty in epitome—
Those hours are best; for those belong
To the lucidity of song.

The Midlands

BLACK in the summer night my Cotswold hill
       Aslant my window sleeps, beneath a sky
Deep as the bedded violets that fill
   March woods with dusky passion.   As I lie
Abed between cool walls I watch the host
   Of the slow stars lit over Gloucester plain,
And drowsily the habit of these most
   Beloved of English lands moves in my brain,
While silence holds dominion of the dark,
Save when the foxes from the spinneys bark.

I see the valleys in their morning mist
   Wreathed under limpid hills in moving light,
Happy with many a yeoman melodist:
   I see the little roads of twinkling white
Busy with fieldward teams and market gear
   Of rosy men, cloth-gaitered, who can tell
The many-minded changes of the year,
   Who know why crops and kine fare ill or well;
I see the sun persuade the mist away,
Till town and stead are shining to the day.

I see the wagons move along the rows
   Of ripe and summer-breathing clover-flower,

47

I see the lissom husbandman who knows
 Deep in his heart the beauty of his power,
As, lithely pitched, the full-heaped fork bids on
 The harvest home. I hear the rickyard fill
With gossip as in generations gone,
 While wagon follows wagon from the hill.
I think how, when our seasons all are sealed,
Shall come the unchanging harvest from the field.

I see the barns and comely manors planned
 By men who somehow moved in comely thought,
Who, with a simple shippon to their hand,
 As men upon some godlike business wrought;
I see the little cottages that keep
 Their beauty still where since Plantagenet
Have come the shepherds happily to sleep,
 Finding the loaves and cups of cider set;
I see the twisted shepherds, brown and old,
Driving at dusk their glimmering sheep to fold.

And now the valleys that upon the sun
 Broke from their opal veils, are veiled again,
And the last light upon the wolds is done,
 And silence falls on flocks and fields and men;

And black upon the night I watch my hill,
  And the stars shine, and there an owly wing
Brushes the night, and all again is still,
  And, from this land of worship that I sing,
I turn to sleep, content that from my sires
II draw the blood of England's midmost shires

Cotswold Love

BLUE skies are over Cotswold
    And April snows go by,
The lasses turn their ribbons
    For April's in the sky,
And April is the season
    When Sabbath girls are dressed,
From Rodboro' to Campden,
    In all their silken best.

An ankle is a marvel
    When first the buds are brown,
And not a lass but knows it
    From Stow to Gloucester town.
And not a girl goes walking
    Along the Cotswold lanes
But knows men's eyes in April
    Are quicker than their brains.

It's little that it matters,
    So long as you're alive,
If you're eighteen in April,
    Or rising sixty-five,
When April comes to Amberley
    With skies of April blue,
And Cotswold girls are briding
    With slyly tilted shoe.

Moonlit Apples

AT the top of the house the apples are laid in
rows,
And the skylight lets the moonlight in, and those
Apples are deep-sea apples of green. There goes
  A cloud on the moon in the autumn night.

A mouse in the wainscot scratches, and scratches,
  and then
There is no sound at the top of the house of men
Or mice; and the cloud is blown, and the moon
  again
  Dapples the apples with deep-sea light.

They are lying in rows there, under the gloomy
  beams;
On the sagging floor; they gather the silver
  streams
Out of the moon, those moonlit apples of dreams,
  And quiet is the steep stair under.

In the corridors under there is nothing but sleep.
And stiller than ever on orchard boughs they keep
Tryst with the moon, and deep is the silence, deep
  On moon-washed apples of wonder.

Elizabeth Ann

THIS is the tale of Elizabeth Ann,
　　Who went away with her fancy man.

Ann was a girl who hadn't a gown
As fine as the ladies who walk the town.

All day long from seven to six
Ann was polishing candlesticks,

For Bishops and crapulous Millionaires
To buy for their altars or bed-chambers.

And youth in a year and a year will pass,
But there's never an end of polishing brass.

All day long from seven to six—
Seventy thousand candlesticks.

So frail and lewd Elizabeth Ann
Went away with her fancy man.

You Bishops and crapulous Millionaires,
Give her your charity, give her your prayers.

Blackbird

HE comes on chosen evenings,
   My blackbird bountiful, and sings
Over the gardens of the town
Just at the hour the sun goes down.
His flight across the chimneys thick,
By some divine arithmetic,
Comes to his customary stack,
And couches there his plumage black,
And there he lifts his yellow bill,
Kindled against the sunset, till
These suburbs are like Dymock woods
Where music has her solitudes,
And while he mocks the winter's wrong
Rapt on his pinnacle of song,
Figured above our garden plots
Those are celestial chimney-pots.

Mystery

THINK not that mystery has place
In the obscure and veilèd face,
Or when the midnight watches are
Uncompanied of moon or star,
Or where the fields and forests lie
Enfolded from the loving eye
By fogs rebellious to the sun,
Or when the poet's rhymes are spun
From dreams that even in his own
Imagining are half-unknown.

These are not mystery, but mere
Conditions that deny the clear
Reality that lies behind
The weak, unspeculative mind,
Beyond contagions of the air
And screens of beauty everywhere,
The brooding and tormented sky,
The hesitation of an eye.

Look rather when the landscapes glow
Through crystal distances as though
The forty shires of England spread
Into one vision harvested,

Or when the moonlit waters lie
In silver cold lucidity ;
Those countenances search that bear
Witness to very character,

And listen to the song that weighs
A life's adventure in a phrase—
These are the founts of wonder, these
The plainer miracles to please
The brain that reads the world aright ;
Here is the mystery of light.

Mrs. Willow

MRS. THOMAS WILLOW seems very glum.
Her life, perhaps, is very lonely and hum-drum,
Digging up potatoes, cleaning out the weeds,
Doing the little for a lone woman's needs.
Who was her husband ? How long ago ?
What does she wonder ? What does she know ?
Why does she listen over the wall,
Morning and noon-time and twilight and all,
As though unforgotten were some footfall ?

" Good morning, Mrs. Willow." " Good morning,
    sir,"
Is all the conversation I can get from her.
And her path-stones are white as lilies of the wood,
And she washes this and that till she must be very
    good.
She sends no letters, and no one calls,
And she doesn't go whispering beyond her walls ;
Nothing in her garden is secret, I think—
That's all sun-bright with foxglove and pink,
And she doesn't hover round old cupboards and
    shelves

As old people do who have buried themselves :
She has no late lamps, and she digs all day
And polishes and plants in a common way,
But glum she is, and she listens now and then
For a footfall, a footfall, a footfall again,
And whether it's hope, or whether it's dread,
Or a poor old fancy in her head,
I shall never be told ; it will never be said.

Deer

SHY in their herding dwell the fallow deer.
   They are spirits of wild sense. Nobody near
Comes upon their pastures. There a life they live,
Of sufficient beauty, phantom, fugitive,
Treading as in jungles free leopards do,
Printless as evelight, instant as dew.
The great kine are patient, and home-coming sheep
Know our bidding. The fallow deer keep
Delicate and far their counsels wild,
Never to be folded reconciled
To the spoiling hand as the poor flocks are ;
Lightfoot, and swift, and unfamiliar,
These you may not hinder, unconfined
Beautiful flocks of the mind.

Passage

WHEN you deliberate the page
    Of Alexander's pilgrimage,
Or say—" It is three years, or ten,
Since Easter slew Connolly's men,"
Or prudently to judgment come
Of Antony or Absalom,
And think how duly are designed
Case and instruction for the mind,
Remember then that also we,
In a moon's course, are history.

History

SOMETIMES, when walls and occupation seem
    A prison merely, a dark barrier
Between me everywhere
And life, or the larger province of the mind,
As dreams confined,
As the trouble of a dream,
I seek to make again a life long gone,
To be
My mind's approach and consolation,
To give it form's lucidity,
Resilient form, as porcelain pieces thrown
In buried China by a wrist unknown,
Or mirrored brigs upon Fowey sea.

Then to my memory comes nothing great
Of purpose, or debate,
Or perfect end,
Pomp, nor love's rapture, nor heroic hours to
    spend—
But most, and strangely, for long and so much
    have I seen,
Comes back an afternoon
Of a June
Sunday at Elsfield, that is up on a green

Hill, and there,
Through a little farm parlour door,
A floor
Of red tiles and blue,
And the air
Sweet with the hot June sun cascading through
The vine-leaves under the glass, and a scarlet fume
Of geranium flower, and soft and yellow bloom
Of musk, and stains of scarlet and yellow glass.

Such are the things remain
Quietly, and for ever, in the brain,
And the things that they choose for history-making
    pass.

To One I Love

AS I walked along the passage, in the night,
beyond the stairs,
In the dark,
I was afraid.
Suddenly,
As will happen you know, my dear, it will often
happen.
I knew the walls at my side,
Knew the drawings hanging there, the order of
their placing,
And the door where my bed lay beyond,
And the window on the landing—
There was even a little ray of moonlight through
it—
All was known, familiar, my comfortable home;
And yet I was afraid,
Suddenly,
In the dark, like a child, of nothing,
Of vastness, of eternity, of the queer pains of
thought,
Such as used to trouble me when I heard,
When I was little, the people talk
On Sundays of " As it was in the Beginning
Is Now, and Ever Shall Be. . . ."

I am thirty-six years old,
And folk are friendly to me,
And there are no ghosts that should have reason to
    haunt me,
And I have tempted no magical happenings
By forsaking the clear noons of thought
For the wizardries that the credulous take
To be golden roads to revelation.
I knew all was simplicity there,
Without conspiracy, without antagonism,
And yet I was afraid,
Suddenly,
A child, in the dark, forlorn. . . .
And then, as suddenly,
I was aware of a profound, a miraculous under-
    standing,
Knowledge that comes to a man
But once or twice, as a bird's note
In the still depth of the night
Striking upon the silence . . .
I stood at the door, and there
Was mellow candle-light,
And companionship, and comfort,
And I knew
That it was even so,

That it must be even so
With death.
I knew
That no harm could have touched me out of my
        fear,
Because I had no grudge against anything,
Because I had desired
In the darkness, when fear came,
Love only, and pity, and fellowship,
And it would have been a thing monstrous,
Something defying nature
And all the simple universal fitness
For any force there to have come evilly
Upon me, who had no evil in my heart,
But only trust, and tenderness
For every presence about me in the air,
For the very shadow about me,
Being a little child for no one's envy.
And I knew that God
Must understand that we go
To death as little children,
Desiring love so simply, and love's defence,
And that he would be a barren God, without
        humour,
To cheat so little, so wistful, a desire,

That he created
In us, in our childishness . . .
And I may never again be sure of this,
But there, for a moment,
In the candle-light,
Standing at the door,
I knew.

The Toll-Gate House

THE toll-gate's gone, but still stands lone,
In the dip of the hill, the house of stone,
And over the roof in the branching pine
The great owl sits in the white moonshine.
An old man lives, and lonely, there,
His windows yet on the cross-roads stare,
And on Michaelmas night in all the years
A galloping far and faint he hears . . .
His casement open wide he flings
With "Who goes there?" and a lantern swings
But never more in the dim moonbeam
Than a cloak and a plume and the silver gleam
Of passing spurs in the night can he see,
For the toll-gate's gone and the road is free.

A Lesson to My Ghost

SHALL it be said that the wind's gone over
 The hill this night, and no ghost there?
Not the shape of an old-time lover
Pacing the old road, the high road there?
By the peacock tree, the tree that spreads its
 branches
Like a proud peacock's tail (so my lady says),
Under a cloudy sky, while the moon launches
Scattered beams of light along the dark silences?
I will be a ghost there, though I yet am breathing,
A living presence still in tight cottage walls,
Sitting by the fire whose smoke goes wreathing
Over fields and farmyards and farmyard stalls.
As a player going to rehearse his faring,
I will send my ghost there before my bones are dust,
Bid it learn betimes the sock it shall be wearing
When it bids the clay good-bye as all ghosts must.
Hush, then; upstairs sleep my lady and her
 mother;
The cat curls the night away, and will not stir;
Beams of lamp and beech-log cross one another,
No wind walks in the garden there.
Go, my ghost, it calls you, the high road, the
 winding,

Written by the moonlight on the sleeping hill;
I will watch the ashes, you go finding
The way you shall walk for generations still.
The window-latch is firm, the curtain does not
    tremble,
The wet grass bends not under your tread,
Brushing you shake not the rain from the bramble,
They hear no gate who lie abed.
Nodding I stare at the hearth, but I see you,
My half-wit travels with you the road;
There shall be your kingdom when death shall free
    you,
When body's wit is neither leash nor goad.
Past the peacock branches proudly gliding,
Your own ghost now, I know, I know,
You look to the moon on the hill-top riding,
The mares in the meadow sleep as you go.
Your eyes that are dark yet great for divining
Brood on the valleys of wood and plough,
And you stand where the silver flower is shining
Of cherry against the black holly bough.
Rehearse, O rehearse, as you pass by the hedge-
    rows,
Remembrance of all that was my bright will,
That so my grave of whispers and echoes

May rest for the ghost that is yet on the hill.
The primroses burn and the cowslips cover
The starry meadows as heaven is clad;
Learn them all, O ghost, as a lover,
So shall your coming again be glad.
The inn-sign hangs in the windless watches,
You pass the shadowy piles of stone
Under the walls where the hawthorn catches
Shapes from the moon that are not its own.
Wander, wander down by the cresses,
Over the crest of the hill, between
The brown lych-gate and the cider-presses,
Past the well and across the green.
Heed me, my ghost, my heir.   To-morrow
Or soon, my body to ash must fall.
Heed me, ghost, and I shall not sorrow—
Learn this beauty, O learn it all.
Night goes on, the beech-log's ended,
Half-wit's drowsy, and doctrine done,—
Ghost, come home from the road; befriended
My moon shall be when I leave the sun.

The Dying Philosopher to His Fiddler

COME, fiddler, play one tune before I die.
Philosophy is barren, and I lie
Untouched now by the plagues of all the schools,
And only silly fiddlers are not fools.

Bring then your bow, and on the strings let be,
In this last hour, merely the melody
Of waves and leaves and footfalls hazardous,
Where crafty logic shall not keep with us.

The patient fields of knowledge did I sow ;
I have done with knowledge—for I nothing know,
Wisdom and folly set their faces hence,
And in their eyes a twin-intelligence.

Only your notes may quick again the keen
Tree-shadows cut upon the paddock's green,
The pools where mirrored branches are at rest,
The heron lifting to her windy nest.

And these are things that know not argument,
Come, fiddler, play ; philosophy is spent.
Out of my thought the chiding doctors slip,
And you are now the only scholarship.

Two Ships

THE morning shone with April on
  A little silver ship at sea,
With happy sails, and bearing bales
To Panama from Tripoli,
    And fortunately bound
    She went without a sound.

Into the night, orlornly bright
There came a little ship of gold,
Without a name, she passed in flame,
With cargoes never to be told,
    Out of a port unknown,
    Swinging to death alone.

Portia's Housekeeping

WE are thrifty of joy in this our modern house;
  We probe the springs of joy with uneasy rods
And shadow the worm in every thrilling bud.
Virtue we know will walk in seedy rags
Of knavery when the better humour fails ;
And we know the good man's shadow of desire.

It was not so with Portia.   She was simple,
Plain for clear yes or no and good or bad.
Bassanio at Belmont in the evening,
Walking the terrace with Antonio,
Was a good man with his friend, and that was all,
Save that his lips were young and masterful.
She had no fine philosophy of sin ;
You lied, and that was bad.   You gave your word,
And, when time came, redeemed it.   A treasure
    kept
At another's cost was ashes in your hand.
She liked her roses red, her lilies white,
And counted punctual hours in guests a virtue.
Sometimes she thought of a Jew and a young
    doctor
Standing before the majesty of Venice,
And smiled, without approval, then again
To sow the asters or feed guinea-fowl.

Gratiano, finding ever new Nerissas
Among her maids, she told not to be tedious,
And Gratiano said she was growing dull.

She liked the verse Lorenzo took to writing
And made some tunes herself upon the lute
To fit a little moonlight sequence.   When
Launcelot Gobbo stole a goose at Christmas,
She did not say he was an honest fellow,
But rated him and almost sent him off;
He didn't brag about it to his fellows.
She had two children, and said two were enough,
And loved them.   She believed there was a God
With an impatient ear for casuistry.
Bassanio had no regrets, but some
Agreed with Gratiano.   I do not know.
In Belmont was a lady richly left?

In the Valley

LET none devout forgive my sin
  Who have not sinned as I;
The soul immaculate within
  Has not to measure by
  My sorrowing husbandry.

The dark, the error, of my days
  Shall be consoled by none
That have not in forbidden ways
  Wandered as I have done
  With faces from the sun.

Princes of virtue, keep your skill
  Of pardon for your peers;
Frail with the frail I travel still
  Along uncertain years—
  Forbear your holy tears.

One hour in black Gethsemane
  I walked with him alone.
He sees, he knows, he touches me—
  How shall it then be known
  To you, O hearts of stone?

Who were before Me

LONG time in some forgotten churchyard earth
  of Warwickshire,
My fathers in their generations lie beyond desire,
And nothing breaks the rest, I know, of John
  Drinkwater now,
Who left in sixteen-seventy his roan team at
  plough.

And James, son of John, is there, a mighty plough-
  man too,
Skilled he was at thatching and the barleycorn
  brew,
And he had a heart-load of sorrow in his day,
But ten score of years ago he put it away.

Then Thomas came, and played a fiddle cut of
  mellow wood,
And broke his heart, they say, for love that never
  came to good . . .
A hundred winter peals and more have rung above
  his bed—
O, poor eternal grief, so long, so lightly, comforted.

And in the gentle yesterday these were but
    glimmering tombs,
Or tales to tell on fireside eves of legendary
    dooms ;
I being life while they were none, what had their
    dust to bring
But cold intelligence of death upon my tides or
    Spring ?

Now grief is in my shadow, and it seems well
    enough
To be there with my fathers, where neither fear
    nor love
Can touch me more, nor spite of men, nor my own
    teasing blame,
While the slow mosses weave an end of my
    forgotten name

Samplers

IN praise of love, upon my mind
   Samplers I'll make to be,
As lovers long ago designed
   Emblems of courtesy,
Threading in warm and frosty wools
Their wisdom's calendars and rules.

He errs to think those hands were set
   All spinster-like and cold,
Who spelt a scarlet alphabet,
   And birds of blue and gold,
And made immortal garden-plots
Of daisies and forget-me-nots.

The bodkins wove an even pace,
   Yet these are lyrics too,
Breathing of spectral lawn and lace,
   Old ardours to renew,
For in the corners love would keep
His fold among the little sheep.

So I will samplers make as well,
   Nor shall the colours lack
In shining characters to tell
   Your lovely Zodiac,
And all your kisses there and words
Shall spring again as flowers and birds.

The Pledge

WHEN love is bright and whole again,
    I'll sing like the bee's weather,
I'll set my colours up again
    Like the cock-pheasant's feather,
I'll find a note to make me one
With lyric birds that sing the sun.

I'll fill my songs with palmer's buds
    And sprigs of thorn for Whitsunday,
And they shall dance as willow rods
    And shine with garlands of the may,
I'll be a theme that takes the spring
From bushes where the blackbirds sing.

I'll walk among my sheep again
    And turn my steps to numbers,
When love is bright and whole again
    And fear has gone to slumbers,
With wings again and flowers and stars
To be my coloured calendars.

Nunc Dimittis

I HAVE seen the plover's wing,
  And the grey willow bough,
The sandy bubbling spring,
The hawk over the plough,
  And now, instructed so,
  I am content to go.

Songs of the lake and wood
Of water and wind I have heard,
And I have understood
According to Thy word.
  What then is now to learn?
  Seaward, O soul, return.

Though I shall walk again
Nor spring nor winter field,
Yet surely in my brain
Are spring and winter sealed.
  Earth you have shown me all,
  I am ready for the call.

Persuasion

Then I asked: "Does a firm persuasion that a thing is so, make it so?"

He replied: "All Poets believe that it does, and in ages of imagination this firm persuasion removed mountains; but many are not capable of a firm persuasion of anything."

BLAKE'S *Marriage of Heaven and Hell.*

I

AT any moment love unheralded
     Comes, and is king.   Then as, with a fall
Of frost, the buds upon the hawthorn spread
Are withered in untimely burial,
So love, occasion gone, his crown puts by,
And as a beggar walks unfriended ways,
With but remembered beauty to defy
The frozen sorrows of unsceptred days.
Or in that later travelling he comes
Upon a bleak oblivion, and tells
Himself, again, again, forgotten tombs
Are all now that love was, and blindly spells
His royal state of old a glory cursed,
Saying " I have forgot," and that's the worst.

II

IF we should part upon that one embrace,
And set far courses ever, each from each,
With all our treasure but a fading face
And little ghostly syllables of speech,
Should beauty's moment never be renewed,
And moons on moons look out for us in vain,
And each but whisper from a solitude
To hear but echoes of a lonely pain,—
Still in a world that fortune cannot change
Should walk those two that once were you and I,
Those two that once when moon and stars were
    strange
Poets above us in an April sky,
Heard a voice falling on the midnight sea,
Mute, and for ever, but for you and me.

This nature, this great flood of life, this cheat
That uses us as baubles for her coat,
Takes love, that should be nothing but the beat
Of blood for its own beauty, by the throat,
Saying, you are my servant and shall do
My purposes, or utter bitterness
Shall be your wage, and nothing come to you
But stammering tongues that never can confess.
Undaunted then in answer here I cry,
" You wanton, that control the hand of him
Who masquerades as wisdom in a sky
Where holy, holy, sing the cherubim,
I will not pay one penny to your name
Though all my body crumble into shame."

Woman, I once had whimpered at your hand,
Saying that all the wisdom that I sought
Lay in your brain, that you were as the sand
Should cleanse the muddy mirrors of my
      thought;
I should have read in you the character
Of oracles that quick a thousand lays,
Looked in your eyes, and seen accounted there
Solomons legioned for bewildered praise.
Now have I learnt love as love is. I take
Your hand, and with no inquisition learn
All that your eyes can tell, and that's to make
A little reckoning and brief, then turn
Away, and in my heart I hear a call,
"I love, I love, I love"; and that is all.

WHEN all the hungry pain of love I bear,
And in poor lightless thought but burn and burn,
And wit goes hunting wisdom everywhere,
Yet can no word of revelation learn,
When endlessly the scales of yea and nay
In dreadful motion fall and rise and fall,
When all my heart in sorrow I could pay
Until at last were left no tear at all,
Then if with tame or subtle argument
Companions come and draw me to a place
Where words are but the tappings of content,
And life spreads all her garments with a grace,
I curse that ease, and hunger in my heart
Back to my pain and lonely to depart.

VI

Not anything you do can make you mine,
For enterprise with equal charity
In duty as in love elect will shine,
The constant slave of mutability.
Nor can your words for all their honey breath
Outsing the speech of many an older rhyme,
And though my ear deliver them from death
One day or two, it is so little time.
Nor does your beauty in its excellence
Excel a thousand in the daily sun,—
Yet must I put a period to pretence,
And with my logic's catalogue have done,
For act and word and beauty are but keys
To unlock the heart, and you, dear love, are
    these.

VII

Never the heart of spring had trembled so
As on that day when first in Paradise
We went afoot as novices to know
For the first time what blue was in the skies,
What fresher green than any in the grass,
And how the sap goes beating to the sun,
And tell how on the clocks of beauty pass
Minute by minute till the last is done.
But not the new birds singing in the brake,
And not the buds of our discovery,
The deeper blue, the wilder green, the ache
For beauty that we shadow as we see,
Made heaven, but we, as love's occasion brings,
Took these, and made them Paradisal things.

THE lilacs offer beauty to the sun,
Throbbing with wonder as eternally
For sad and happy lovers they have done
With the first bloom of summer in the sky,
Yet they are newly spread in honour now,
Because, for every beam of beauty given
Out of that clustering heart, back to the bough
My love goes beating, from a greater heaven.
So be my love for good or sorry luck
Bound, it has virtue on this April eve
That shall be there for ever when they pluck
Lilacs for love.   And though I come to grieve
Long at a frosty tomb, there still shall be
My happy lyric in the lilac tree.

WHEN they make silly question of my love,
And speak to me of danger and disdain,
And look by fond old argument to move
My wisdom to docility again,
When to my prouder heart they set the pride
Of custom and the gossip of the street,
And show me figures of myself beside
A self diminished at their judgment seat,
Then do I sit as in a drowsy pew
To hear a priest expounding th' heavenly will,
Defiling wonder that he never knew
With stolen words of measured good and ill,
For to the love that knows their counselling,
Out of my love contempt alone I bring.

Not love of you is most that I can bring,
Since what I am to love you is the test,
And should I love you more than any thing
You would but be of idle love possessed,
A mere love wandering in appetite,
Counting your glories and yet bringing none,
Finding in you occasions of delight,
A thief of payment for no service done.
But when of labouring life I make a song
And bring it you, as that were my reward,
To let what most is me to you belong,
Then do I come of high possessions lord,
And loving life more than my love of you
I give you love more excellently true.

WHAT better tale could any lover tell
When age or death his reckoning shall write
Than thus, " Love taught me only to rebel
Against these things,—the thieving of delight
Without return ; the gospellers of fear
Who, loving, yet deny the truth they bear,
Sad-suited lusts with lecherous hands to smear
The cloth of gold they would but dare not wear.
And love gave me great knowledge of the trees,
And singing birds, and earth with all her flowers,
Wisdom I knew and righteousness in these,
I lived in their atonement all my hours ;
Love taught me how to beauty's eye alone
The secret of the lying heart is known."

THIS then at last; we may be wiser far
Than love, and put his folly to our measure,
Yet shall we learn, poor wizards that we are,
That love chimes not nor motions at our
    pleasure.
We bid him come, and light an eager fire,
And he goes down the road without debating,
We cast him from the house of our desire,
And when at last we leave he will be waiting.
And in the end there is no folly but this,
To counsel love out of our little learning,
For still he knows where rotten timber is,
And where the boughs for the long winter
    burning,
And when life needs no more of us at all,
Love's word will be the last that we recall.

THE END

INDEX OF FIRST LINES

93

CPSIA information can be obtained
at www.ICGtesting.com
Printed in the USA
LVHW081233240322
714285LV00004B/45

9 781375 424806